CW00983290

STORIES FROM THE
BIBLE

Om
KIDZ

An imprint of Om Books International

OmKIDZ|Om **Books International**

Corporate & Editorial Office
A-12, Sector 64, Noida 201 301
Uttar Pradesh, India
Phone: +91 120 477 4100
Email: editorial@ombooks.com
Website: www.ombooksinternational.com

Sales Office
107, Ansari Road, Darya Ganj
New Delhi 110 002, India
Phone: +91 11 4000 9000
Email: sales@ombooks.com
Website: www.ombooks.com

© Om Books International 2013

Retold by Subhojit Sanyal

ALL RIGHTS RESERVED. No part of this book may be reproduced or transmitted in any form by any means, electronic or mechanical, including photocopying and recording, or by any information storage and retrieval system, except as may be expressly permitted in writing by the publisher.

ISBN: 978-93-81607-93-0

Printed in India

10 9 8 7 6 5 4 3

Contents

The Story of Creation

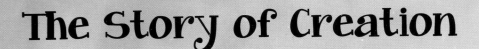

In the beginning, God created heaven and earth. Looking at earth, he then said, "Let there be light" and suddenly the entire earth was washed with bright light all around.

Seeing the sparking bright light everywhere, God declared, "We shall henceforth, call the shining light 'day' and the deep and dark shall be called 'night'"

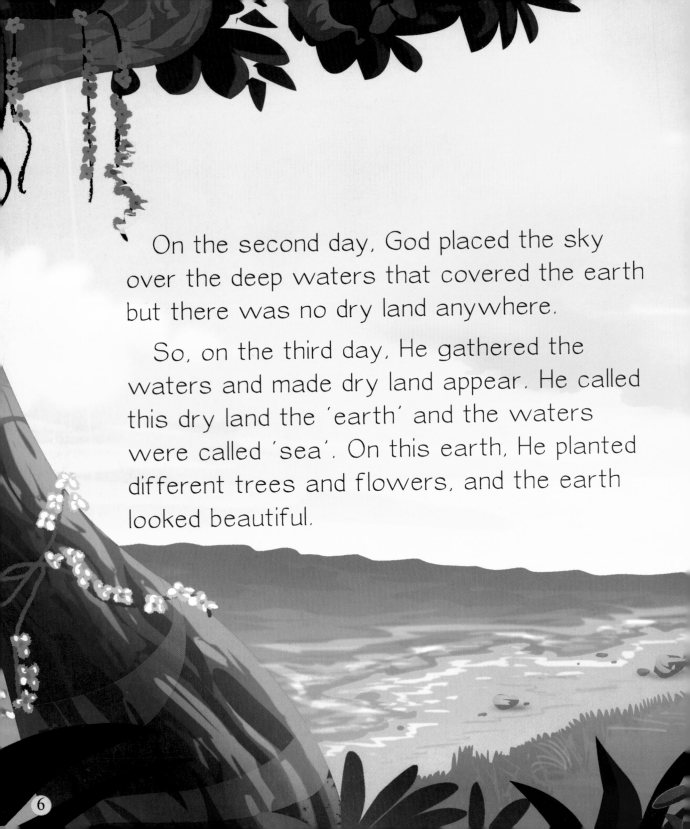

On the second day, God placed the sky over the deep waters that covered the earth but there was no dry land anywhere.

So, on the third day, He gathered the waters and made dry land appear. He called this dry land the 'earth' and the waters were called 'sea'. On this earth, He planted different trees and flowers, and the earth looked beautiful.

On the fourth day, God decided to make great lights appear in the sky. In a moment, He made the sun, moon, and stars.

When the fifth day came, He filled the oceans and seas with living creatures — whales, dolphins, fishes, and the sky with beautiful birds of all colours and kinds.

On the sixth day, He placed animals on the earth — elephants, lions, monkeys and even ants and mosquitoes. When the earth was full, He decided to make people after His own image.

When the seventh day dawned, God saw that the whole universe had been completed. So He rested. He blessed the seventh day, and made it holy.

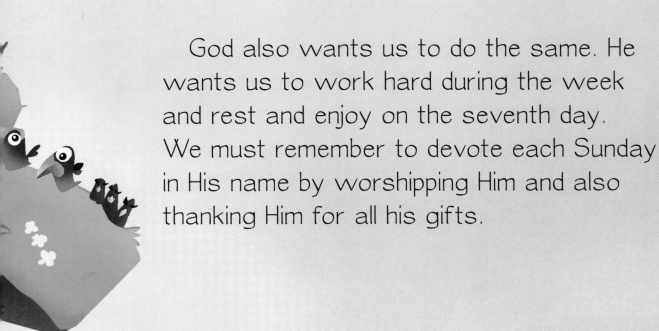

God also wants us to do the same. He wants us to work hard during the week and rest and enjoy on the seventh day. We must remember to devote each Sunday in His name by worshipping Him and also thanking Him for all his gifts.

Adam and Eve

When God first made earth, He realised that there was no one to take care of it. He took a lump of clay from the ground and formed it into a man. Then God bent down and breathed life into the man.

When the man came to life, God named him Adam. He wanted Adam to be happy, so He planted a beautiful garden with apple, pear, mango, fig, and many other trees. Right in the middle of the garden, He planted two trees — the Tree of Life and the Tree of Knowledge of Good and Evil. The garden was named Eden.

The garden was beautiful and God told Adam to enjoy the fruits of all the trees, except for the fruits of the Tree of Knowledge of Good and Evil.

Adam was obedient, and lived happily in the beautiful garden God had made for him.

But Adam was lonely and God saw this and felt sad. One day, when Adam was sleeping, He took out a rib from Adam. From this rib, He made a woman and finally Adam was happy. He called the woman Eve.

Adam and Eve lived happily together in the beautiful Garden of Eden.

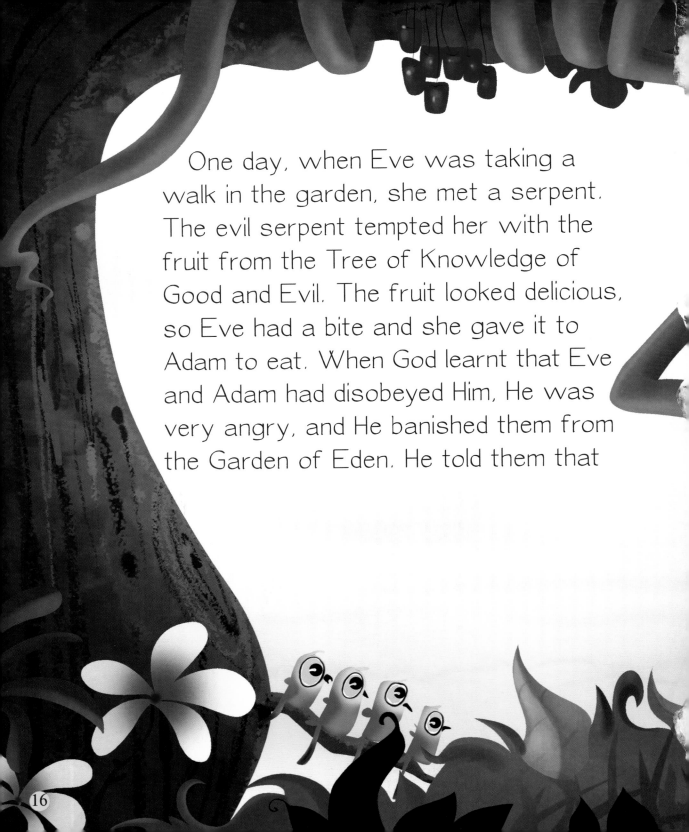

One day, when Eve was taking a walk in the garden, she met a serpent. The evil serpent tempted her with the fruit from the Tree of Knowledge of Good and Evil. The fruit looked delicious, so Eve had a bite and she gave it to Adam to eat. When God learnt that Eve and Adam had disobeyed Him, He was very angry, and He banished them from the Garden of Eden. He told them that

they would have to work hard and face many difficulties in life along with their children. But, even though God was angry with them, He loved them and wanted them to learn the lesson of Life.

Cain and Abel

Even though Adam and Eve had sinned, God still loved them very much. He blessed them with a baby. This was the first baby ever born. They named him Cain. After that, they had another baby and they named him Abel .They had other children too after

Cain and Abel. Their children had children and their children's children had children. And that is how the world began to be filled with people.

When Cain grew older, he became a farmer and when Abel grew up he became a shepherd and looked after sheep.

One day, Cain and Abel brought gifts to God to thank him for all the good things He had done for them. They built an altar for a sacrifice to be made. Cain brought some of the things he had grown like wheat, figs and grapes. Abel brought the first lamb born to one of his sheep. God was happy with Abel's gift because He knew Abel wanted to please Him. But He wasn't happy with Cain's gift, because He wasn't sure whether Cain would do what He wanted. This upset Cain very much. Cain blamed Abel for this. He wanted to take revenge, so he called Abel out to the fields and killed him with a rock.

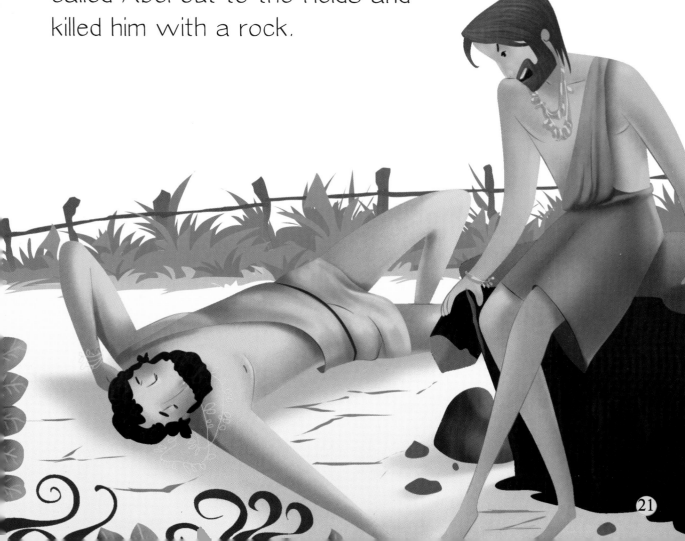

God found out what Cain had done and He told him that, as he had spilled Abel's blood on the ground, the ground wouldn't grow his crops anymore. He would have to go far away to find food. Cain was afraid that his

relatives would find out what he had done and kill him. God put a mark on him, so that people would know that God was protecting Cain. However, he had to leave and go away to a distant land.

The Story of Noah

Many, many years had passed, and the world forgot all about God. Earth became as bad as Hell. God was watching all this, and saw that no one cared about doing anything good anymore. But amongst all this evil, He saw one good man — Noah.

Noah still loved God and tried to do what God said. Finally,

God told Noah that He wanted to finish the mess people had made of this world and start all over again. In order to do so, He asked Noah to build a huge boat (He called it an ark). Noah told God that he couldn't do the work alone, so God told him not to worry as He was with him. So, with God's help, Noah started building the ark. He worked day after day for many years till one day the ark was ready. Then God

asked Noah to find two of every kind of animal, a male and a female, and bring them back to the ark. God also told him to get enough food for all the animals. With God's help, Noah was able to get all the animals, and just as he was placing the last animal into the ark, it started to rain.

God then told Noah to get into the ark with his family. There was his wife, and three sons and their wives. Then God reached down from the Heavens and shut the door of the ark.

It rained and rained for forty days and forty nights, and Noah's ark floated above the highest mountains. There was no dry ground and everything that lived on earth, died.

Noah and his family waited in the ark. For 150 days the ark was tossed on the waves. They wondered if God had forgotten them. No, God hadn't forgotten His children. One day, a warm wind started to blow, the rain stopped and the water began to go down. It took another 150 days, till the water receded

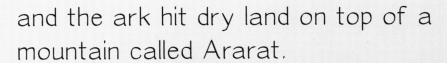

and the ark hit dry land on top of a
mountain called Ararat.

Noah sent a dove out to see if it could
find land. Seven days later, the dove came
back with a fresh olive leaf in its beak.
Land had been found, and an olive bush
had started growing on
dry land.

Finally God told Noah that it was time to leave the ark. They rushed out to find new homes in the world that God had washed clean.

God had saved them!

After the animals trooped out of the ark to fill the earth again, Noah picked up rocks and built an altar. Then Noah sacrificed some animals to God in order to thank Him. God was very pleased with the sacrifice and promised Noah that he would never destroy the world again with a flood. He set a rainbow in the sky, which would be a sign of the promise between Noah and God.

The Story of Moses

The story of Moses takes place where the people of Israel were living in captivity. They were called the "Hebrews". They had to work hard for the Egyptians, but the Egyptians were afraid of them, as they were multiplying fast, and it looked like there would be more Hebrews and less Egyptians soon.

The cruel Egyptian Pharaoh passed an order wherein all the male children born to Hebrew slaves had to be killed.

One day, a Hebrew woman named Jochebed gave birth to a boy. They tried to keep the baby hidden, but as he grew and started making noises, they knew that the soldiers would find him and kill him.

This baby had an older sister, named Miriam. She had an idea. She made a special basket that would not sink in the water. Then she took the basket to the edge of the river, and placed her brother in it. The basket floated among the reeds, and the baby slept contentedly. Before they let the baby go, they gave it one last kiss and prayed to God to protect the little child from the cruel soldiers.

The Pharaoh's daughter came to the river for her daily bath. The little baby in the basket had woken up and was feeling hungry. He started to cry and soon the princess found the baby in the basket among the reeds.

The princess picked him up and cuddled him, as he was such a beautiful baby.

Miriam, the baby's sister had been watching all this from a distance. She ran over to the princess, and asked her if she would like to use the services of a woman who could nurse the baby and love him, as her own. Naturally, the princess immediately agreed, and soon Jochebed

was put in charge of the baby. She was grateful to God, and knew that God had special plans for her child.

When the baby grew older, the princess took the baby to live in her palace. She planned to raise him like an Egyptian prince and she named him Moses, which meant that he was drawn from the water.

God Gives Moses the Ten Commandments

Moses grew up to be a deeply religious man and had immense faith in God. God selected him to deliver the Hebrews from their misery.

As Moses reached Mt. Sinai, directed by God, he realised that he was on Holy Land. He removed his sandals and went closer to a burning bush he saw there. Then he heard God's voice. God told him that He wished to give the Hebrews ten laws (or Commandments), by which they should live.

You shall have no other Gods before me.

You shall not make for yourselves an idol.

You shall not misuse the name of the Lord.

Remember the Sabbath Day by keeping it holy.

Honour your Father and Mother.

You shall not murder.

You shall not commit adultery.

You shall not steal.

You shall not give false testimony against your neighbour.

You shall not covet.

These Commandments were hewed on rock with God's finger of fire. Moses thanked God for His mercy and grace, and carried the stone slabs on which the Commandments were written, down the slopes of Mt. Sinai.

The Story of Balaam and his Ass

Balaam was travelling on his ass, heading to a place where God did not want him to go. When he was on his way, God sent an angel with a sword to stop him. Balaam did not see the angel but his ass saw it. Therefore, he took a side road. Since Balaam had not seen the angel he whipped the ass soundly.

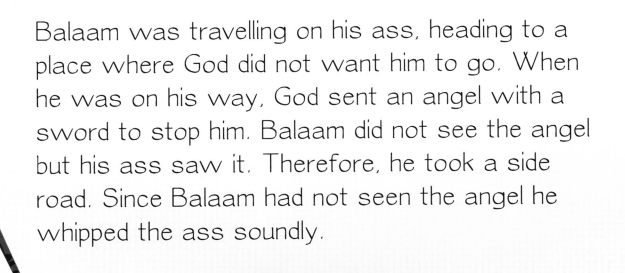

The road was a little narrow with vineyards on one side and a wall on the other. As they were passing, the ass saw the angel with the sword again. To save his master, he took another narrower road but Balaam scraped his leg against the wall. Again Balaam whipped the ass.

As they were going through the narrow lane, the ass saw the angel once again. He was about to move when Balaam whipped him so hard that he fell on the ground. Then God gave the ass the ability to speak to Balaam.

The ass told Balaam that each time he had moved to a narrower road, it was only because he had seen the angel with the sword coming to kill Balaam.

Unfortunately, instead of thanking him, Balaam had whipped him again and again. Balaam, realised his mistake and looked after his ass properly after this.

Samson the Brave

There came a time, when
the people of Israel forgot their
God. The cruel Philistines ruled over them
and treated them like slaves. One day, a slave
woman had a dream in which an
angel appeared and told
her that she would

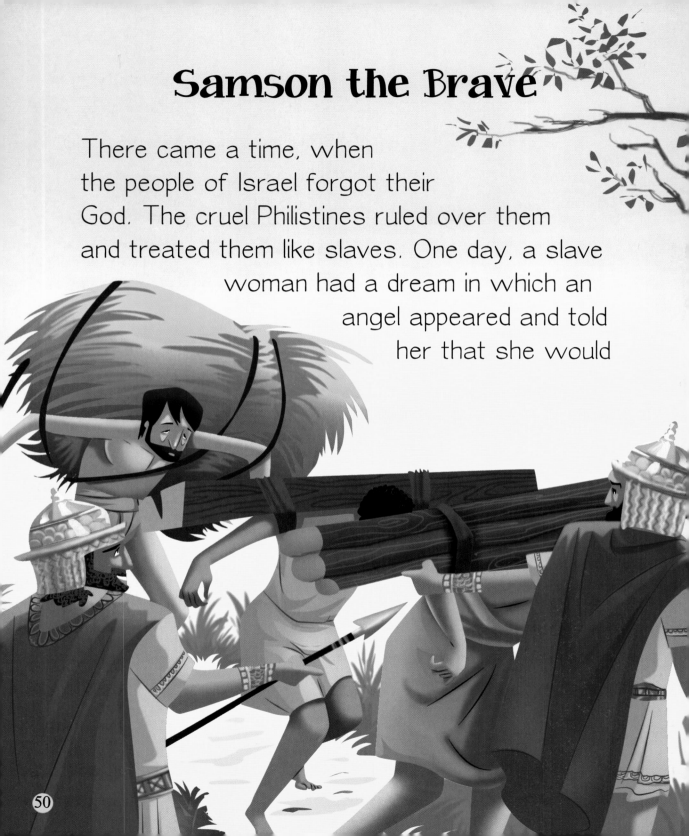

soon become a mother. Her son would grow to be brave and very strong but she was never to cut his hair. The secret of his strength was in his hair.

When the son was born, he was named Samson; he was tall and strong and very brave. As a young boy, he showed his courage when he fought a lion which had attacked him. In no time at all, Samson tore the lion apart with his bare hands.

God was with Samson and he did many mighty deeds.

However, the Philistines had also heard about Samson and were scared of him so they sent an army to find him. But the power of God was with Samson and he killed one thousand men and defeated the Philistine army.

The Philistine kings were getting tired of Samson. He was leading his people to disobey

the rulers. Now they decided to find out the secret behind his immense strength.

They went to his beautiful wife, Delilah, and offered her 1100 pieces of silver. In return, she was to tell them the secret of his great strength.

Even Delilah did not know, so she used all her charms to find out. Day after day, she pleaded with Samson and one day he finally told her the secret of his strength.

Now, this was Samson's greatest mistake. That night when Samson

slept, Delilah cut off his long hair. The Philistines came the next morning to a Samson who was weak so they caught him, tied him up in chains, and dragged him away. Then they blinded him with hot pokers. Poor Samson was now blind and weak and had to work for hours every day.

Slowly, as time passed, Samson's hair started growing back. The Philistine kings had forgotten their prisoner and were feasting and celebrating their victory over Samson. One day, he was dragged to the great temple and made to stand between the two columns which supported the temple. The temple was filled with the Philistine people, who were making fun of him and his God.

Samson prayed to God asking for strength. Then he pushed the two columns on both sides and the great temple came crashing down on him and all the other evil people who were there.

Even though Samson died, it was his final victory over the Philistines.

David and Goliath

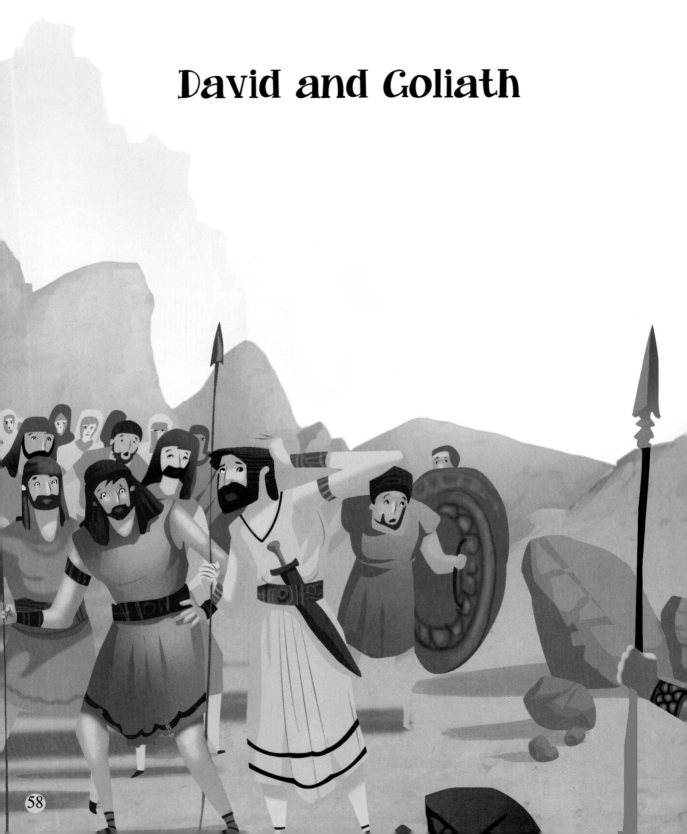

The Philistine army was at war with the Israelites. However, there was terror in the ranks of the Israeli army. This was due to a giant Philistine named Goliath. He was nine-feet-tall, and when he walked, the ground shook. For 40 days, the two armies waited for the other to make the first move. Goliath would come

to the field, shouting and cursing the Israeli God. One day, David came to the battlefield and heard Goliath shouting and defying the Israelis. David was a young shepherd boy but he was pure at heart and his faith was strong. He asked King Saul to allow him to face the Philistine giant on the battlefield.

Goliath came on to the battlefield, dressed in full armor, with spear and javelin. David came dressed in his shepherd's clothes, carrying a sling and a bag of rounded pebbles. When Goliath saw this, he was very amused, but

David took
out a stone, held it to
his sling and asking
for God's help, he
released the stone.
The stone
hit Goliath
on the centre of
his forehead. When
Goliath fell down,
David took out

Goliath's sword and cut off his head.

When the Philistine army saw that their hero was dead, they fled, leaving the field to the victorious Israeli army.

This young boy, one day, became King David.

Wise Solomon

Solomon, the son of David, became the wisest man on earth. People came from all over to ask him questions. Even great kings and queens came to meet him and brought him beautiful gifts.

One day, two women came to him with a baby boy. The women said that they lived in the same house and that

each had a baby but they showed up with only one baby! Now, both women claimed it to be their own. They wanted King Solomon to tell them who could keep the little baby.

Solomon had a wise plan. He asked for a sword and told the servants

to cut the baby in half, saying that he would give each woman half a baby. He was not really going to harm the baby but he wanted to see what the women would do. He knew that the baby's real mother would not let her son die.

One woman told Solomon to cut the baby in half, but the other woman loved the child, and told Solomon not to do so but give it to the other woman.

Solomon now knew who the real mother was. He gave it to the

woman who had begged him not to cut the baby and the other woman was punished.

This is how King Solomon showed his wisdom.

The Story of Job

Job was a good man who was rich. He had a wife, ten children and many animals. He obeyed God's Commandments and God had given him many blessings. God knew Job was righteous, and so did Satan, but Satan felt that Job was virtuous because God had

given him so many blessings. He thought that Job would not be so virtuous if his blessings were taken away. God claimed that Satan could take away everything that Job had but he could not hurt Job, and Job would still be righteous. One day, Job's oxen and servants were killed; his sheep were burnt, his camels stolen.

A strong wind blew
down his son's house,
his children were killed.
He had nothing left but he
was not angry with God. He
worshipped God and told Him
that he had nothing when he

was born; God had given him everything, now God had taken it away. He still loved God. God spoke to Satan again, and told him, that though everything had been taken away from Job, he was still righteous. Satan said that he would not be righteous if he were very sick. God knew that Satan could make him

sick but he could not kill him. Job became very sick; his body was covered with sores but Job still had faith in God. His friends came to visit him. They told him that God punished wicked people and so Job must have been wicked. Job told them that he had not been wicked and did not know why so many evil things were happening to him. He said that he could die but he would always love God. If he did die, he would be resurrected; he would have his body back again and he would again see God. Then Job heard the voice of God

who asked him many questions. Job answered all these questions and certain things that he did not understand. God told Job that men could not always understand why God did certain things. Men must trust God, no matter what

happened to them. Then Job saw God. Job had been righteous through all his troubles. Job loved and trusted God.

God blessed Job and gave him more than he had before. God gave him more animals. Job and his wife had many more children and they were very happy. Job lived to be a very old man.

OTHER TITLES IN THIS SERIES

 9 789381 607725

 9 789381 607381

 9 789383 202775

 9 788187 107811

 9 788187 107828

 9 789381 607442

 9 789381 607367

 9 789380 069760

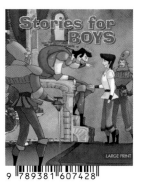 9 789381 607428

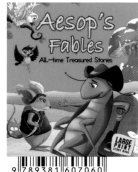 9 789381 607060

 9 789381 607275

 9 789381 607206

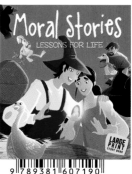 9 789381 607190

 9 788187 107965

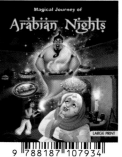 9 788187 107934

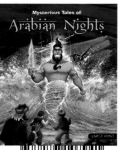 9 788187 107941

 9 788187 107927

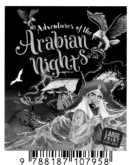 9 788187 107958